CHICAGO
Role Model Publishing
2019
It's Not Regular: How to Recognize Injustice Hidden in Plain Sight?
by Jahmal Cole

Books may be purchased by contacting the publisher and author at: jcoleofrmp@gmail.com

Cover Design & Layout: Vince "ST!ZO" Wasseluk
Images captured by Jahmal Cole and Leon Peatry
Images edited by Yolanda Richards
Role Model Publishing LLC.
Editor: Patti Mckenna
ISBN: ISBN: 978-0-578-54161-7.
Education 2. Self Help 3. First Edition
Printed in USA

D1082611

TABLE OF CONTENTS

To the city that brought out my fire,
been fighting out of the Chatham corner for the last twelve years.

3   **IT'S NOT REGULAR**

It's not regular to have to order food through three-inch bulletproof glass windows. If you just ordered your quiche through a bulletproof glass window, you'd be traumatized. Can you imagine ordering a medium-rare steak at Gibson's through a bulletproof glass window? This is why kids feel they have to yell to get what they want. They are taught at an early age to yell to get their food.

BULLETPROOF GLASS WINDOWS

"The blue bag, the blue bag." Those are the words a lady yelled to the Eastern European man standing behind the bulletproof glass window. There isn't a microphone and the glass is three inches thick, so customers have to yell their orders through the window. "No, not the spicy nacho, I want the cool ranch. The blue bag, the blue one!"

This morning, there was a long line outside of the bulletproof glass windows at the gas station on 75th and Stony. I was about fifth in line, so I had a lot of time to think about things. I thought about the mug shot photos taped to the bulletproof glass and how there are always black faces staring back at me on the windows. Black faces like mine, wanted for violation of parole, murder with intent to kill, writing bad checks, failure to pay child support. This is what students see on their walk to school in the morning. I want to sue, or at least challenge, this newspaper and convince them to put up some shots of a black engineer at Facebook, a black business owner, or a black anthropologist.

While in this long line outside of the bulletproof glass window, I noticed that the owner or employee looked tired, but safe with an illusion of security. When the salesman finally came back with the blue bag of Doritos, he passed change to a lady through the sliding bulletproof glass door. It was like he was a prison officer passing food through a slot in a cell door to a prisoner in solitary confinement. The environment I was in at that gas station felt like I was in jail, but I was free. By the time it was my turn to shout my order through the three-inch bulletproof glass, I hesitated and stopped, becomingly suddenly aware that if I shopped at this gas station, I'd be subsidizing my own failure. Yelling my order through the thick glass would mean I agreed or at least accepted, the fact that this was the norm. I don't agree with it, and I don't accept it. I know that things like this affect our everyday lives. They affect our kids, who grow up believing it's normal. It affects our kids, who learn what they live. And what have they learned? To shout, because thick bulletproof glass has taught them to yell to get what they want.

I asked a kid what he did over the weekend. He responded, "Jahmal, I had a good time. I got to travel a little bit; got to see a lot of my friends and family. We ate great food, got to dress up and hear some good music. I had a blast."

I said, "Wow, man! I can tell by your expression that you had a great time. Where'd y'all go, to Six Flags or something?" The kid responded, "Oh, no. We went to Leaks on 79th. It was the best funeral I've ever been to."

If this could be the cover of this book, it would. People getting buried in fake Louis Caskets. Talk about going out in style.

THE YOUNG TWO-SKIE

The helicopter flying over my house is my alarm clock. By now, police car sirens have long ago become white noise. And the ambulance drivers are courteous—they don't turn their sirens on after 11 pm. They still flash their blue and red lights; maybe that's protocol, but they don't turn on their sirens. I know they're there, though, because I can hear their engines zooming by. It doesn't matter what time of day or night it is, the helicopters never forget how to make a grand entrance; they make my house shake. Time to get up.

Just an overwhelming presence of police in our communities. It's actually offensive.

I love my morning jogs down and around 79th Street. Nothing too serious, just a quick two, three miles. Young two-skie is what I call them. The other day, a white butterfly floated east with me from Michigan to Prairie. I felt like it was an angel, because I leave my house knowing I can be shot down while out jogging. I hate writing this, but that's just the reality out here. I'm not stuck on it too much, though. I'm still going to go out jogging; I'm just saying that I do feel the heaviness of carrying the burden of having to be so aware. It's like jogging with a backpack.

My friend always says, "Hey, signs and symbols." It could happen, man. I pray it doesn't. I swear I don't want to put that energy out there, but as we say in Chicago, "any and everything can happen to you out here."

I don't even watch scary movies, nor would I consider sky diving or anything like that. My real life is enough; I don't need more thrills, excitement, or risks. Pumping gas at night without being robbed is a win. Being hungry at night and going to Subway and making it back home without incident is a win. You have to be aware when walking out of the house.

You have to be.

I've seen a lot over the past ten years. Once you've been shot at seven times on a sunny day, you never can relax again. So it ain't like I'm going to go out jogging and forget about being shot at. I'll get into more later, but I'll just say that what appears to be a calm block with manicured lawns can turn into a tragedy in an instant. You always have to be on alert, and after a few years, you don't even realize that you're carrying the burden of being aware. It's like a backpack, maybe even ankle weights. Even when you take the weights off, you're stronger, no longer a virgin, and the bad news just becomes the news. The worry becomes compartmentalized. Nothing is ever too much for you because you've seen and heard it all. Maybe that's what PTSD means.

Pops used to tell me that his mom used to say, "People can be so angry they sleep with their fists balled up." It's true also that teens on 71st and Jeffery can be so cautious they walk with one hand in their hoodie pocket, even if they don't have a gun. They just want the wolves to know that it could go up if it has to. "Let a nigga try me, try me."

I can relate; I slept with a knife until I was 25 years old. I got that from Grandma Helen, back in Ft. Worth, Texas. During her whole life, she slept next to a shotgun on the side of her bed. Someone asked me how I stopped sleeping with my knife—well, I started sleeping next to my gun and the Bible. I flipped the switch off safety after saying grace and had an extra clip loaded just in case.

Yeah, it's safe to say that I'm on edge. There's a thin line between sanity and PTSD. When calm days become almost too calm, my antenna goes up. My pops says to never leave the house without having a plan, or you'll probably be a part of someone else's plans. I guess this dangerous reality is never too far from my conscious. I'm telling you, right when you relax, man, right when you pull out your phone while walking in Englewood is when the shooting happens. That one time when you don't look over your shoulder at the gas pump is right when that robbery happens. Satan is waiting to pounce. He lulled you to sleep, thinking you've tamed the devil. Things aren't so bad out here. Yeah, right.

You just can't get away from the murder talk. You can't turn on the news or go to the barber shop without hearing about somebody being killed. There didn't used to be a lock on the barber shop door, but nowadays, they have to know you before you get buzzed in. If they don't know you, the barber will say, "We only take appointments." It's not safe around here, man. Everybody is strapped. Can't trust a soul, really. People just keep their 38 in the hoodie pocket, forget about a holster.

Maybe we all suppress the fear; maybe we're all desensitized to the sound of gunshots. No, that feels cool to write, but I've never met anyone that numb or calloused to the sound of gunfire. The best you can hope for is to be experienced enough to return fire. You watch videos of people being shot on the block and the little kids know exactly how to react in a block shooting. They tell the victim to keep breathing and yell, "Stay woke, stay woke! Somebody call the police." I'm telling you, they are experienced in this drama.

You tell me. I really have no clue what this means.

Shit, I'm actually woke as hell. I'm overly antsy after all my incidents and war stories.

One time, while out with my daughter at a playground in Hyde Park, I heard a gunshot that came from Lake Shore Drive. Shit, I didn't need any announcements, I knew the drill. I dropped to the ground real fast. Then, in one instant, like I was doing an up-down drill at football practice, I sprang right back up to my feet and ran to grab my daughter, and pulled her to the ground and covered her up. We stayed that way for about ten seconds. I didn't hear any more shots, nor did I hear any screams. I checked myself and my daughter, and we were both okay. When I stood up, the park was noticeably empty. There really wasn't anybody outside but my daughter and me.

Damn, that might have just been a tire popping on Lake Shore Drive, I thought. But I don't work at Michelin. How would I know? I suppose that's a plausible scenario. Maybe I'm just too antsy. But since I didn't have any visible proof, and there really isn't time to play out all these scenarios in the moment, I just reacted.

To stop my daughter from being traumatized, I had to play it off and not let her see the fear in my eyes. I just acted like I was playing in the wood chips.

I thought, "Shit, you're in Hyde Park, Jahmal. That's exactly why you came to the park over here, to be somewhat safe and stay away from the shootings." I'm ashamed to say that I don't even let my daughter ride a bike down my street anymore, especially now that guys are starting to congregate on the porches and stray German shepherds are running loose like it's regular out here.

There is more technology on the light poles than there is in the classrooms.

I know you're probably thinking, "Well, Jahmal, how come you don't just move? Or, how come you don't just call the police?"

Well, number one, I'm not moving, and number two, I call the police and tell them that there are 15 guys sitting on the front porch, drinking and smoking and telling war stories. They tell me that congregating on the porch isn't illegal. Well, let me tell you that getting 15 people to come to a block club meeting is tough. How the hell can the house across the street get 15 people to show up every day between 12pm and 4pm? Whoever runs that house is an excellent community organizer.

Because of all these extracurricular activities, when we go to the park, we travel a few communities away, somewhere that I can feel safe enough to be with my daughter.

I really hope no one from the high rises that overlook Burnham Park saw me running and diving to the ground. That video would probably be funny ... or tragic. Depends on who you show it to. Maybe they were real gunshots, though. I have no clue.

Nowadays, there really are people shooting at the park, and they ain't shooting fadeaways. They don't bank at Chase, but every day is another paper chase. Metaphorically, I've looked over my shoulder so much my neck is cramped. This is the South Side of Chicago—you know, you watch the news.

But I still go running in the mornings. The young two-skie. I touch fists with the old heads as I pass through the blocks. I say good morning to the people at the bus stops.

The first turn from Wabash is on 79th at the Taylor Funeral Home. That's where my run usually begins and gets real. The sun rises in the east, and I love the beams on my face. I remember hating the sun as a child because I was teased for being so dark, but now I love the sun. I'm comfortable running toward it. I quickly snap back to reality when I hear the crackles from stepping on broken bottles on the ground as I pass the methadone clinic.

As I near MLK, the aroma of weed reminds me of my childhood and growing up listening to Gil-Scott Heron in the house as my pops cleaned up. My pops ain't never stopped smoking weed. He smoked it his entire life. These days, smoking weed is legal, but for Pops, it was always legal. He rolled his joints in zig zags and rolls two together somehow, still does.

I throw up the peace sign to all the cops and bus drivers. I just want to thank them for their service, like I'd thank somebody who served in the military. Thank you for agreeing to serve and protect us imperfect human beings. I know people hate on the cops because some of them make some questionable decisions, but it's relative, man. Some countries don't have a police station or fire department. Having a police badge gives you a platform that allows your true character to show. If you're a good person, having a badge gives you a platform to do good. If you're a bad person, having a badge gives you a platform that'll amplify your wickedness. I still wave what's up or throw a quick salute when I pass by.

Back to my young two-skie, as I'm jogging, I make it a point to say good morning to everybody, but not the drug dealers. I act like I don't see them. The city shows me love, and I return it like Devin Hester.

The entire bar waves at me as I pass the 40 Cafe, which opens at 7 a.m. I guess it's for the people who just got off the third shift. For them, it's really 10 p.m. I ain't mad at them. I used to need a drink to calm myself down, too. Ciroc vodka was my favorite getaway. It was a $30 vacation from my problems. I stopped drinking a year ago though, after hearing Malcolm say, "Every time you break the seal on that liquor bottle, that's a government seal you're breaking." I guess that line started to make sense to me, coupled with the fact that I started seeing liver dialysis type hospitals everywhere. I took that as a clear sign that I shouldn't be drinking anymore. My friend always talks about the signs and symbols of the conscious mind. I'm beginning to pay attention.

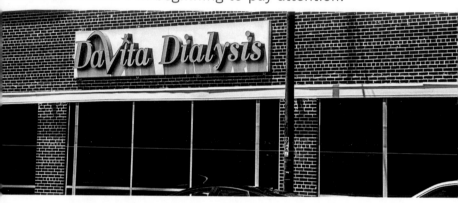

As I round the corner on Cottage near Happy Liquors, I know I'm halfway home. I speed up a little bit before the final stretch. This is usually when I start smelling barbecue chicken in the air. Smells so good. Whitney Young Library is now renovated. Years ago, I was an advocate for those renovations. I guess ten years is an accurate temporal unit to expect a city to put a library in place. I now know how long the government takes to update a library.

Every time I pass Captain Hard Times, I think of the time we fed homeless and welcomed 30 Africans from 30 different African countries. From Cape Verde to Botswana, Uganda to Zimbabwe, we all ate chicken and waffles right here on 79th Street. It wasn't those north side gluten-free chicken type waffles, either. I'm talking real chicken wings and Louisiana sauce.

Sometimes while I'm running, I count the amount of boarded-up buildings within a three-mile radius. I lose count after 1.5 miles, having already counted 16 boarded up businesses. I also struggle with wondering what constitutes a boarded up business. Do bars count as boarded up businesses? To me, it feels and looks like the entire block is in jail. Pro line door systems are making a killing in Chicago. Every business on the block is caged up at night.

Chicago doesn't assign red "X" signs to just any vacant or abandoned building; a sign is a visual cue that a structure is structurally unsound and that firefighters and other first responders should take precautions when responding to emergencies there. It's also an extra reminder for anyone who might wander into a vacant building that they should stay out. These signs are basically mayday calls to the community to stay out. I don't think seeing big red X's is good for my spirit. It feels like I'm being marked for a drone bombing. Plus it's just confusing because the city didn't let anyone know why they were putting these X's on homes. Nobody's going to do anything about this community, as a last ditch effort, let's just put a big red X on the building—that's doing something, you know.

Sometimes as I run, I can't even look across the street because I know there's drug dealing going on. The dealers see me almost every morning, and I attribute my safety to the fact that I don't really go around witnessing too much. There's really not much to see; it's more of a feeling that I get when I jog by.

It's the same feeling I used to get when I was seven or eight years old and my dad would park outside of the dope house to go and get his Saturday morning high. He'd leave me in the car in the hood for ten or twenty minutes, and I'd be so scared of my surroundings. I'm not really sure why I was scared; all hoods don't look scary, some hoods look like upstanding blocks. But I believe dope houses give off a certain energy, maybe because so many souls and hopes are trapped inside. As I jog down Cottage Grove, I can tell which are the drug houses. I can feel it.

When I pass by what used to be Chatham Foods, I think about when they sold my book about community organizing. They didn't charge me any money or take a percentage. The owner just loved what I stood for. It wasn't even the money that was a blessing; I was just happy to be getting my name out there.

The fire station starts my final sprint. When I get home, I'm all good. I said I'd be back in 20 minutes, and it took me 19 and some change, but you never know out here.

Just never seen this before.
To me, #ItsNotRegular.

Kids can't be safe when they're walking to school nowadays. They don't even call it walking to school; they call it going on a mission. Every other corner has a big yellow sign that reads "Safe Passage." Safe Passage is a program where the Chicago Public Schools pays $500,000 per week for people to stand along the routes where kids walk to school to ensure they will be safe. When I grew up, they were called crossing guards and were there to protect kids from traffic. Nowadays, they're called Safe Passage base operators, like a military base. Same terminology as the kids use when they say they're in the field, in the trenches, at war with the opposition. These Safe Passage base operators wear green safety vests with class three reflective tape. I just want to give you a picture of what your kids are processing on the walk to school every day.

BE SAFE

I was grabbing my morning coffee at Kusanya Cafe in Englewood, as I do almost every morning, and the lady behind the counter passed me my coffee in a to-go cup. As she slid me the coffee, she said, "Be careful." I said, "What, is the lid not on properly? Is there not a coffee sleeve on the cup to insulate my hand from the heat?" She said, "Oh no, I meant be careful when you walk outside today. It's crazy out there. Be careful."

Her comment made me step back and think because I wasn't expecting a "have a nice day" at all. I'm actually used to guys at the barbershop saying, "Alright man, be safe."

But as a society we've progressed from saying "have a nice day" to the courteous alert of saying "be safe," and now we've elevated that caution to saying "be careful." Next year when somebody slides me a coffee, they'll say, "Look out!! Duck!"

Be safe, be careful. In some parts of the country, they say, "Be easy." That word "be" is so POWERFUL! Most of us don't think of the word "be" as an action verb. We think of the word be or being as being effortless, right. You don't wake up in the morning and say, First, I just have to be, then I gotta jump on the train, then I just have to be, then I have to go to work." No, you don't say that; you just assume you're going to "be" okay.

Not in Chicago. In Chicago, we can't even take just "BEING" for granted. Just pumping gas at night is a gamble for your life. We ask ourselves, "Do I stop and get gas at 11:30 at night or, or should I just risk running out of gas on the e-way?" That's a good question to ask if you care about your

well-being in Chicago. I know how I'd answer it. Personally, I ain't stopping at 63rd and Lafayette for gas at night.

And the Shell gas stations have to stop asking for phone numbers and emails at the gas pumps, too. Y'all trying to collect all this consumer data and don't even have any lights on the poles. The pumps run slow and trickle out gas, debit card buttons aren't working at all, but you want my phone number. It's too risky, man, and that's just pumping gas.

You also have to be careful when you call an Uber to take you to the airport. The uber driver shows up to your house and asks, "Are you going to Midway? You're going on vacation huh? Well, how long will you be gone?" Then while he has you in the car, he'll text message his friend, who will go to your home and clean you out.

Do I call an uber from my

house or have them pick me up down the block? That's a good question to ask if you care about your well-being in Chicago.

Walking to school isn't safe in Chicago, either. Kids don't even call it walking to school; they call it going on a mission. Every other block has a big yellow sign that says "Safe Passage. Safe passage is a multimillion-dollar program by the public schools, where they pay people to stand outside on the routes where kids walk to school. When growing up, we called them crossing guards. Nowadays, they're called Safe Passage Base Operators, like a military base.

It's the same terminology the kids use when they say they are "in the field," or "in the trenches," or "going to war with the opposition."

These are Safe Passage "base operators" that wear lime-green safety vests with Class 3 reflective tape (worn on the side of the road by construction workers or by people who work in hazardous conditions). They take up a position on the routes where kids walk to school every day. They want them to be safe.

I'm not hating on the efficacy of the program. My goal is for you to visualize what kids have to process on their walk to school every day. They're learning more on the walk to school than they're learning in the school.

If you were walking down the street and saw a sign that said, Caution: Grizzly Bear in Area, would you risk it and stay? Or would you say there was no way you were going to walk down that street? That's how it is with the school's safe passage areas. I don't care how good the school is, I'm not sending my kid down that path to school every day. It isn't safe.

IT'S NOT REGULAR

COUNTERFEIT MARKER

I've never seen a real counterfeit bill. I'm sure they exist, and there are people with fancy printers who can probably print watermarks, but I've never seen one of these bills, nor do I think it's worth my time to learn how to work a counterfeit bill print printer, if that even exists. If you're going to take the time to learn a skill that produces an illegal end product, you might as well invest in a Microsoft administration class and learn about computer hardware. Seems like it's just as difficult a trade, but has a better return.

The same could be said about selling weed. In high school, I saw lots of friends breaking down weed, sometimes grinding it down with a fancy grinder, measuring it all out on triple beam scales that they'd ordered online. I had a cousin who found fake weed in a field behind his apartment complex. He said it wouldn't get you high at all, but he'd

I recently wondered why the hell I trust the cashier if they don't trust me. What's stopping them from giving me counterfeit money? The next time they hand me a twenty-dollar bill, I'm going to say, "No offense, but wait one second while I pull out my fancy counterfeit detector pen."

grab a lot of it, put it on defrost in the microwave, and then break it up and add this stuff to the regular weed. I don't know how much he could stretch with this process, but I thought it was genius. I've also heard rumors of some folks using oregano to beef up their weed.

I had a friend who used to break out his triple beam scale for measurements and bagged the weed in little baggies. Thinking back on this, I didn't really have the level of appreciation I should for his craftsmanship. This kid had ordered a digital scale and took the time to really learn how it works.

I saw his report card once, and he had received straight F's. I always thought it was impossible to get straight F's, but he did that successfully. But he was smart enough to use two humidors and different processes for purple weed and red hair weed. He'd put the red hair berma in a humidor and the purple weed in the refrigerator. I honestly thought it was too much geekiness. And this was just his preselling, sifting and bagging. He hadn't even gone outside yet. I'm not even getting into the actual bagging of the weed and separating the nickels and dimes, and eights and halves and quarter ounces and pounds, etc. In high school, I didn't know enough about math to sell weed, so I just played basketball.

After all that hard work, I wonder if anybody ever asked him to check the measurements of a dime bag of weed. How much is a dime bag supposed to weigh? Is it even an ounce? Would someone give it the eyeball test and let you slide if you were a few ounces off? Feel free to laugh. I told you I wasn't smart enough to sell weed. I was out learning how to crossover dribble and catch a football—you know, easy shit. Anyway, would my friend take offense to someone checking the weight of his weed?

I don't know. I know one thing, I've never been offended when the cashier at the corner store slows down the line and holds my twenty-dollar bill up to the light and looks for the security strip embedded in the paper to the left of Andrew Jackson.

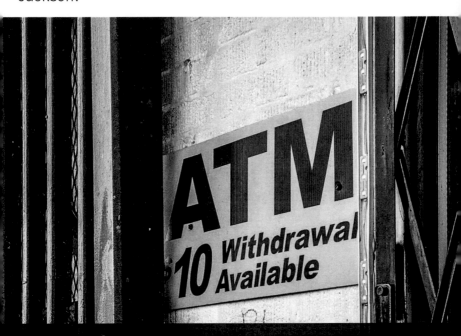

I was hoping to show you that these ATM's actually have a $30 withdrawal limit, but now they have $10 ATM withdrawals. I feel like the fees are at least $2.50, so when you take out $10, the bank executives are laughing all the way to the bank.

Some cashiers even take it a step further when you hand them a fifty-dollar bill or a hundred. That's when they get fancy and pull out the yellow highlighter. It's actually called a counterfeit detector pen. They cost about $10 on Amazon. Basically, it's a pen that contains iodine solution that reacts when it comes into contact with the starch in wood-based paper and creates a black stain. When the solution is applied to regular fiber-based paper used in real bills, no discoloration occurs.

I don't know why I'm not offended when the cashier does this. They sit behind the bulletproof glass window and check your money. That's a double whammy. They're basically saying, I'm too scared to serve you without this barrier between us, and I don't trust you or the money you're handing me. This process is so regular that I'm not one bit inconvenienced, nor do I feel disrespected by the process.

I recently wondered why the hell I trust the cashier if they don't trust me. What's stopping them from giving me counterfeit money? The next time they hand me a twenty-dollar bill, I'm going to say, "No offense, but wait one second while I pull out my fancy counterfeit detector pen."

I really don't know anybody knows what the acronym EBT stands for. We know what it means, but do we know what the acronym stands for? It actually stands for Electronic Benefit Transfer, which is an electronic system that allows state welfare departments to issue benefits via magnetically encoded payment cards. That's what the acronym stands for, but what does this sign mean when you see it? Would this sign be out of place on the door of a Whole Foods or a fancy grocery store?

IT'S NOT REGULAR

WOLVERINES JACKET

An older black gentleman wearing a Wolverine jacket came into the coffee shop this morning. When I saw the jacket, it reminded me how much I loved those colors as a kid. Michigan University was my favorite college basketball team; maybe they still are. To me, they represented the cool kids, and I wanted to be cool like that one day. I complimented the older man on the jacket and asked him if that was his favorite team as a child, too. A shocked look came across his face, and he said, "No, I'm a graduate of Michigan University." Ha! I realized I don't' see people in shirts and think it's their alma-mater. That was a great spark for my writing today. No matter what I experience, my thinking was shaped during a very innocent, but yet ignorant, point in my upbringing. This ain't regular.

Coming up in the hood, we didn't choose clothing based upon affiliations; we chose sports clothing based on which teams we liked. We watched sports highlights all the time, so we knew a lot about all the college and professional teams. We had no clue how to get to a big named school. (I'm not even sure if I knew what a big named school was. We definitely didn't choose a school by what courses it offered, definitely not because of an affordable tuition price. I didn't know the difference between D1, D2, and D3 at all. I suppose a good school to me was a school that was on TV.) We had no lifeline to anyone who had gone to college, and we had never met anybody who had ever been to one of the big named schools. We just watched college basketball on Saturdays. We needed something to do when my dad was smoking weed and cleaning the house. Even today, when I'm walking down the street and smell skunk weed, it smells like Saturday morning college basketball.

The Fab Five and Michigan University were the talk of the talk when I was a kid. Chris Weber, Jalen Rose, wow. The navy and gold jerseys they wore were everybody's favorite colors, as far as basketball was concerned. I remember dreaming of my first car being navy blue with a gold stripe down the middle.

As a child, there was literally no way I was ever going to wear any Michigan University apparel. Yeah, right. My best hope was to find an old jersey at the thrift store that didn't have all the paint chipping from the numbers. I occasionally found these and played in them every day like they were new. To me, they were new.

On Sundays, I wished I could stay home and watch sports like I did on Saturdays. Sunday was even cooler because that's when NFL games were played, but my dad always dressed me in a suit and made me go to the Kingdom Hall of Jehovah's Witnesses with my mom. My dad wasn't big on religion, but he liked that the Hall gave me an opportunity to be a public speaker. "I let you go so you wouldn't be afraid to speak in front of white people," has always been his reasoning.

They were against sports at the Kingdom Hall because it was too much competition. Even college wasn't encouraged. My mom preferred I'd learn a trade. I guess this is why we never talked about college much.

My cousin was a drug dealer, and he used to let me play Bill Walsh football in his bedroom on his Sega Genesis. The first time I ever saw cocaine was when I looked under his bed for a remote control. I remember the cocaine looking pinkish or maybe it was brownish. It definitely wasn't as white as I assumed cocaine to be.

IT'S NOT REGULAR

Anyway, he had all the best games on Sega. On this particular day, I remember playing Bill Walsh football. I think Florida State was the cool team, and I think I always lost to Nebraska. Michigan was also a good team, one reason why I loved the colors.

I come from an area and a mindset where we might see a Michigan University sweater in the mall and purchase it, or we might buy a Kansas University jersey and wear it with the shoes. I was a Purdue fan when growing up, so I once bought a Purdue university sweater. I didn't realize that the people in downtown Chicago would think this wasn't regular, or they'd think I was an imposter. Most people who have college values instilled in them wear college clothes based on their affiliations and their alma mater. I guess they did this in the Cosby Show, as well, but I never even knew what Morehouse or Howard was. I probably thought they were colleges or maybe fraternities, but I never really thought about it because nobody had ever taught me about it.

When I saw the older gentleman wearing the Michigan University jacket, I assumed he was a fan, like me. But I never assumed he was a graduate of the college. By the look on his face and the matter of fact way he responded, I could tell he thought I should have known he was a graduate. His look made me remember where I come from.

BARBER SHOP

My regular barber has been sick, so I've been taking chances and going to random barber shops all over the South Side. A few weeks ago, I found a good barber. He'd already cut my hair once and did a great job. While cutting my hair, he bragged about fine tuning his barber skills while in Statesville prison. He's been in and out of county his whole life, so now the guards know him, and he gets fast tracked through processing. The guards see him now as a mentor of sorts. He could supposedly cut a person's hair with a small razor blade located inside a plastic Bic shaver. "Only thing you hate about jail is that's it's boring as hell," he said.

He worked alone in this shop because his former partner wasn't with him anymore. "You could tell he was dipping in it, he was dippin in it, he'd been dipping in the product" and "then Africans came in and got him. They slit his throat and shot him in the head_____ style." I actually forget the name of the execution style he mentioned ... couldn't find it using the aforementioned details on Google, either.

As you can imagine, he was telling me all of this as he gave me a razor blade lining. My father always told me you have to give a good tip to a person who holds a razor blade to your neck. That advice has always resonated before, but in this moment, it made a lot of sense. Long story long, he did a great job, I tipped him, and he ran outside and asked me, "Do you know how much money you just gave me?" I smiled and said, "Yeah, man, thanks for taking me with no appointment."

That was last week, and my regular barber is still in the hospital, so I had to go back to the barber with the jail stories. I didn't have his number so I walked up to the shop

IT'S NOT REGULAR

and saw him sleeping on the couch. It was about 11:00 a.m., so I decided to knock on the door. The door was covered with so many rusted steel bars, and the way they separated gave me no blunt surface to make a clean knock. I didn't want to knock on the bars because I didn't want him to think it was the cops, and I also didn't want my hand to get cut. Luckily, I saw his number on the door, so I called. When he answered, he sounded like he was still half asleep, which I knew he was. I didn't mention that I saw him sleeping. For all I knew, he might have fallen on hard times and lived in the shop. It wasn't any of my business. I simply asked if he was going to be in the shop today. He said, "Yeah, I'll be there in an hour, stop by then."

I decided to walk around the block. I saw some African dresses in the window of a shop, and I know my lady loves those. As I was walking toward the shop, I passed a neighborhood laundromat. I saw a beautiful woman washing clothes, and I reminisced on my laundromat days. The privileges I take for granted become more apparent as I walk around the hood. To some folks living in South Africa, having a washer and dryer is a privilege and riding a bicycle is a luxury. Poverty in Chicago is upper middle class in South

Africa. It's all relative. I love it, and I'm appreciative.

As I approached the shop with the African dresses, the barber called back and said, "Hey, is this the guy with the big van and works with the kids? Aww, come on by man, I'm in here laying down, figured I'd call and tell you the truth. It was a long night at the shop, you know what I mean."

I had no clue what he meant, but I could only imagine. Maybe the big tip incentivized him to call me back so rapidly.

I told him, "It's all good, bro. I'm going to pick up my lady a dress at the nearby African shop, and I'll come through an hour." I figure I'd give him some time to regroup and wake up. Don't want him giving me a razor blade lining when he's half asleep.

After I hung up, doubt set in, maybe a sharp breeze came by that brought with it a negative memory. Maybe it was a bill that needed to be paid. Oh wait, I remember, my lady raved at the craftsmanship of a guy who made these dresses at the African Festival. She squeezed his arm and told him how awesome he was to start his own brand. She'd never even been to one of my events or talked about my apparel like this, but she does that, so no surprise African dress for her. I guess I'm petty. Maybe I'm in my feelings. She'll have to settle for some surprise Church's Chicken or something.

Seriously, for whatever, I decided to pass on the dress. Instead, I sat in my van for an hour and rearranged some goals. While sitting in my van, I witnessed another barber shop owner and his son walk into a shop directly across the street. There are so many barber shops and beauty supply stores in my community. Word has it that Chatham has the most beauty supply shops in the country. It makes one wonder why the South Side can be so ugly on some days. We spend so much money on external beauty, but very little money on intrinsic beauty, mental health, goal setting, etc.

As these guys were walking into the business, the guy in front opened the door and saw a lady approaching. She was a very small statured lady, maybe in her twenties, but her drug addiction made her look much older. It was clear that she was a drug user and wanted money, but the old man addressed her with compassion and said, "How may I help you, young lady?" Before she could respond, the guy behind the old man reached around and handed her a dollar, without even looking at her. There was no compassion. Like a great quarterback, he'd seen this situation a thousand times. His muscle memory took over as he peeled off a dollar from his wad of money and gave it to her. She walked up the block, and I'd forgotten about her, but a few minutes later she walked back with her head down and at a really brisk pace. Without looking up, she said thank you as she passed the two men, and it dawned on me that she may have just scored drugs from somewhere close. The two men didn't say anything as she passed them, but I wondered if they had just subsidized her failure.

BUCKET BOYS

"Ain't selling no drugs or nothing." That's what the bucket boy told me as I pulled up to the light at 87th and Lafayette. That was his sales pitch.

I rolled down my window and said, "What?" He said, "Yeah, man, I ain't selling no drugs or nothing."

I responded, "So the fact that you're 'not selling drugs' automatically qualifies you to be paid. The bucket boy said, "Yeah, ain't like I'm out here trying to rob nobody."

I said, "So, I guess because you aren't robbing me, your entitled to be compensated."

He said, "Yeah, I ain't got no job, ain't nobody hiring cuz I got a felony on my record, plus my parents ain't around. I gotta be the backbone, take care of my little sister, you know."

The backbone he said, take care of his little sister.

Now I'm a student of effective communication, and I'm always judging these bucket boys' sales pitches. I like the "ain't selling no drugs approach" if you're looking to get some ashtray change, but if you want some real money to take care of your little sister, the real question is, why aren't you selling drugs or nothing? Entry-level pharmaceutical reps earn 75k base salary and bonus potential. You clearly don't lack the hustle. The sheer grit and determination of dodging cars off 87th, talking to complete strangers, and making sales presentations before the light turns green demonstrates you having the skills. Why aren't you selling drugs or nothing?

The bucket boy told me, "Man, I'm just out here tryna make some bread because the city is messed up, these gangs are messed up, these cops are messed up." That's when I knew his philosophy was messed up.

I told him, "Hold up, hold up, hold up, disappointments aren't reserved for bucket boys on 87th Street. What about the bucket boys on 35th, 47th, Garfield, 63rd, 69th, 79th, and 95th? Surely it rained on them today, too."

I told him that his problem wasn't money. His problem was not having any idea how to get more money. I asked him to let me see his list of goals. He said he didn't have any. I said, "See, you have to start there. If you don't have a list of goals in your back pocket, I can guess how much money is in your bucket within $25.

I knew that having a list of well thought out goals would change everything for him. So I gave him a journal that had the words "my goals" on the front cover and asked him to write his name on it.

You see, he wasn't suffering from a poverty of finance. No, poverty in Chicago is upper middle class in Mexico. He was suffering from a poverty of imagination, a deficit of hope

But how did he get this way? How does an able-bodied teenager with great courage and presence end up beating on a bucket on 87th and Lafayette? Have we as a community encouraged this behavior by giving them hand-outs? Are we subsidizing their failure? Crippling their minds? As a public, do we have a responsibility for these circumstances? I think we do.

I run an afterschool program for youth and the kids are always saying that they are a product of their environment or they are a victim of their circumstances. I think you're a product of your expectations, but I definitely agree that your environment affects your well-being. I definitely think that environment produces particular outcomes, and the future of our children depends on the physical, mental, and spiritual environments they are in.

We take students from divested community areas on educational field trips; we call them explorations. A lot of students have never been downtown; they've never seen the lake. They've never waived for a taxi. Their entire worldview is shaped by the infrastructure of their neighborhood. In Chicago, that's tragic. We believe exposure is key, so after school, we expose students to different cultures, professions, and even cuisines. At the end of the exploration, we have a 15-passenger van we use to drop the students off at their homes.

For context, I'm the Founder and Executive Director of My Block, My Hood, My City. We're a social impact organization that operates like a mini city hall. We're a social hub of ideas, and we get shit done.

Our "Explorers Program" is for 150 Chicago youth—some might call them disconnected youth. These education reform buzzwords are always changing every season, like the downtown styles: jeans with brown boots and colorful socks. That was in fashion last fall, but maybe it'll be different next year. Anyway, I think "disconnected youth" is still the term that's in vogue, nowadays.

Our mission for the explorer's program is that, "By 2025, no student will ever say they've never been to downtown Chicago and interacted with the business district."

Although our students are teenagers between the ages of 14 and 18, a lot of them have never been downtown Chicago and have never seen Lake Michigan. They've never been on a plane or waved for a taxi. They've never been inside of the new elevators that don't have any buttons, never had a boarding pass, and haven't ever seen a Tesla in real life. If you're driving a Tesla and we're out exploring downtown, expect to be stopped at the light and one of our students will politely ask you if he or she can take a photo while standing in front of your car. Being downtown is literally like a fish-out-of-water experience for many youths we work with.

The explorer's program reinforces my belief that the environment affects well-being." Moreover, environment produces particular outcomes, and the future of our children depends on their physical, mental, and spiritual environments.

CRIME SCENE TAPE

I dropped a student off at their house the other day, and there was yellow crime scene tape wrapped around the alley on the side of her apartment. One of the other kids in the car said, "That's yellow tape, that's regular stuff. It ain't serious because if it was serious there'd be red tape." These were teenagers, but life had taught them all how to be forensic scientists.

I dropped a kid off at 63rd and Western the other day, and he jumped out and ran a block like he was ducking from a shelling. How long does it take to become desensitized to hearing gunshots? Little Eric tells himself they're firecrackers and goes back to sleep. You could be at a backyard cookout with 30 family members, and 50 shots could ring out from an automatic rifle. Everybody would stop talking for a brief second, and then carry on like nothing even happened. This is regular stuff. Things like this happen every day. People get shot at and make sarcastic jokes.

I'm beginning to believe that people watch the news for entertainment. The anchor is usually a beautiful, intelligent, and curvy black woman who delivers the news about the shootings every day. People love the black news anchors in Chicago because they're beautiful. I follow a few of them on Instagram, and I'm always very happy to see that they're on vacation. I think they should take as many vacations as possible because reporting on death and murder year after year takes a toll on you. You have to get away from Chicago for a while to maintain your sanity. I could not imagine being a reporter in the city. You'd probably have to take a six-month break from reporting crime and start reporting music for a couple months. Environment affects your well-being, not only for the students in the hood but for also the working class in Chicago. Activists are definitely going crazy, left and right.

TOO MUCH TRASH

How many times do you have to walk by a vacant lot full of trash before you become completely disengaged? You don't even see the trash anymore or rats as big as Arizona cans. What happens when you push a baby in a stroller past this trash? Does the baby grow up thinking it's regular? The answer is yes. The environment affects your well-being.

I took a group of students to McDonald's the other day, and they all ordered food. All the kids eat is McDonalds. You ask them how far they live from the school, and they'll say they live two McDonalds away. Lol. McDonalds is the distance marker for miles.

Ironically, when I take them out of state and they ask to stop at McDonalds, they all say that the meat tastes better out of state than at the McDonalds in Chicago. What's in the food in Chicago? The kids can definitely taste the difference. It'll take generations before we really know what herbicides and genetically modified hormones are in our food supply.

Anyway, everyone ate their food. Before Kendall got out of the van, I asked him to take the trash with him. He got out of the car, took all of the McDonalds value meal bags, and threw them on the ground like it was a piece of gum. He had no reaction, or any second thoughts. He didn't care. He didn't look back, didn't break stride. He just threw it on the ground like it was regular.

Have you ever been to somebody's home and while watching TV, you see a mouse run by their feet? It happens so fast that you don't even have time to play like you didn't see it.

Then, they see the mouse, too, but they show no reaction

IT'S NOT REGULAR

or physical reflex at all. I'm not expecting an apology or something, but they don't even provide any small talk: "Damn, did you see that mouse? It's crazy, man. This place is going downhill." They don't say anything at all.

Pretty soon, the same mouse comes back out. This time, he brings his friends with him. They say, "Come on out, y'all. It's safe, these people don't mind. They don't have any physical reflexes. They've become used to the decrepitness."

That's just what the drug dealer says in front of the liquor store. They stand out on the community corners in front of the store all month and sell their drugs. The store owner never calls the police. The next month, they tell their friends to come on out, the store owners don't mind, they cool with us selling drugs right here. They won't do anything. They have no physical reflexes. The community is used to the decrepitness.

This is how we are as a community. Our physical reflexes are bad. There are no physical reflexes to pick up trash. No physical reflexes to call the police. A doctor using a reflex hammer to check your reflexes usually hits you in the knee to check for any abnormalities in your central nervous system. If he hits your knee and there's no knee jerk reaction, something is wrong with your central nervous system. Well, there's no physical reflex when they see trash. They see no reason why they should pick it up. And that response does indicate a reflex—a psychological reflex.

What type of psychological reflex do kids have when they walk past 20 boarded up buildings every day? What type of psychological reflex do you have when you have to look over your shoulder every minute for ten years? What type of psychological reflexes are you having when you're on alert and on defense all the time?

There is so much that isn't regular in these schools. There is so much that isn't normal but that we see so much that it has become the new normal. There's no soap, paper towels, sometimes toilet paper in the bathrooms. This echoes the idea that students feel like they are learning in filth.

This is a Culture of Stress, and it produces fight or flight. There is so much adrenaline in our systems that we're always hyped up. When you're hyped up, you can't dream about the future. Simply put, you can't dream when you're in pain!!!!! I went to a funeral the other day, and my student's father was in so much pain that they buried him in a Louis Vuitton casket. My people are in so much pain that we spend $300 on a pair of Jordan's because it makes us feel good, and when we feel good, we don't feel so much pain. Teenage boys and gang members wear Jordan's. Finding something that makes us feel good lessens the pain, at least temporarily.

What type of psychological reflexes occur when you see Section 8 Welcomed signs and Ciroc vodka billboards? Everywhere you look, there are blue lights flashing like it's regular, German shepherds sniff you on the train like it's regular, shot spotters sit on top of poles, listening for gun shots like it's regular, kids order food through bulletproof glass windows like it's regular. They've been doing it so long they don't even notice the bulletproof glass anymore. They don't notice the microphones on top of the poles. It's not regular to walk inside Walgreens and see that all the cough syrup is locked up. It's not regular for the billboards in my community to promote cheap divorces and $6,000 tax advances. It's not regular that we have 15 currency exchanges and one bank. How am I supposed to save? It's not regular for there to be a liquor store on every corner. It's not regular for there to be a holding cell in the basement of a funeral home. It's not regular for there to be two paddy wagons parked outside the front of my high school. It's not regular to have to take off your belt and shoes before walking through the metal detector in a high school. It's not regular for everybody to carry clear book bags. It's not regular to see bright yellow safe passage signs on the walk to school. It's not regular for everyone's parting statements to be "Be Safe." A kid told me the other day that he keeps his phone unlocked just in case he gets shot. He wants someone to be able to contact his people. It's not regular for 80 percent of the students in my program to know someone who was murdered, but only 10 percent know someone who has graduated college.

None of that is normal, but it's becoming so commonplace in our community that it seems regular. Man, the integrity of this city is at risk if we aren't supporting programs like My Block, My Hood, My City.

MY BLOCK
MY HOOD
MY CITY
★ ★ ★ ★

These roll-down gates have become part of the features of the urban business district. Every business has a roll-down steel gate to protect from theft. In the morning, before the businesses open, this looks kind of weird. it looks like a ghost town. When I'm passing by, it'd be nice to see something marketed in the window of the stores. Curb appeal or window shopping isn't even possible in the hoods of Chicago. You just see steel gates.

BRANNOCK DEVICES

I recently stopped in South Shore at a popular shoe destination to buy a pair of sneakers for my daughter. I'd always wanted to stop in this store. I'd noticed the line is usually single file and winds down the block. You can always tell when a new pair of Jordan's are being released. I asked a man working in the store if he had a brannock device to measure the student's foot. He said they didn't have one in the store, but he had a big desert eagle looking pistol on his hip that my six-year-old daughter pointed out. Here we were in a shoe store, and there weren't any foot-measuring instruments around, but there was an armed guard at the front door and an armed guard that floats around to bring you the shoes. Society once again is holding its nose up at you.

SHAQ SHOES

As a kid, the thrift store was my Neiman Marcus. I remember being so proud of finding someone else's hand-me-down gear. I'd go there, hoping I could find a Ninja Turtles t-shirt or a Seattle Super Sonics jersey that was fresh enough to pass as semi new. I wanted so badly to be accepted as a cool kid in school, but it never worked. My clothes never had that new clothes luster. My jeans always appeared washed 700 times, and the screen printed Super Hero logos on my t-shirts always seemed to be chipping.

Payless Shoe store was my Footlocker. One summer, around income tax time, my mom took me to Payless. I spotted a pair of Shaquille O'Neal shoes. They were blue, white, and black. I remember thinking they were the fake Shaq shoes because they were so cheap, and I hated Payless shoes because after a few weeks of playing, small balls of cotton would start to come out of the stitching, and I'd get teased at school. These

Shaq shoes looked different, though, maybe they were made with real leather, I had no clue back then. I just knew they shined and gave off that new shoe luster. All my other clothes appeared washed and well worn, but my shoes shined just enough for me to have some dignity in second grade. Now I still didn't get treated like the kids who had new Jordan's, Grant Hill Filas, or the Jason Kidd's. It wasn't even close, but I was decent for the first time. My Shaq shoes shined just enough to make it till fall arrived. As the seasons changed, I remember seeing those cotton balls start seeping through the stitching at the top of the shoe.

I remember Head Start and food stamp booklets. I remember thinking SpaghettiOs was actually spaghetti. I remember breaking into people's houses to eat grapes, pineapple, and Captain Crunch cereal. The first time I ever tasted lasagna was during a break in. I remember tasting it and feeling rich. The first time I got caught stealing, I stole a trapper keeper and a protractor. I remember my dad being proud of me.

My mom did the best she could. Today, I feel ashamed of having felt so ashamed of walking into Payless and the thrift store. Damn, as I sit next to those clothing donations boxes in the ghetto, I feel Shaquille O'Neal.

My friend says that when you listen to dead rappers, it's devil worship. Hindsight is 20/20. It was a beautiful day in Englewood—one of those winter days when snow is on the ground, but the sun is out, teasing you about springtime. 71st and Morgan appeared calm. I don't remember exactly how I said it in my mind, but I remember thinking something along the lines of, "the media is too hard on Englewood. There are beautiful people, beautiful homes, and great teachers in this area. It's not as bad as they media makes it seem."

There were no parks in front of the school, so I decided to park a block or two down. I'd just hopped out the car, after driving around blasting a mixture of Lil Durk and LA Capone music. I love how they paint pictures of their hoods and the judge not caring about their stories. I don't know, I like listening.

I walked past a park and eventually made it to the corner of 72nd and Morgan. At the corner, I noticed a picture taped on the light pole. The picture was of a kid who had been killed. This must have been a tribute to a young man who had had grown up in the area, or near that block. I stopped at the corner and took a photo of this picture, because I enjoy taking photos of the community as it is. This guy was being honored on his block.

I turned right onto Morgan and walked into a high school, prepared to give a presentation. I work with a lot of alternative schools, now called option schools. Lots of the kids who attend these schools have been kicked out of traditional public school or are coming out of jail. I went into the school to give the presentation, but nobody was expecting me, not the students, not the faculty, nobody. I sat in the gym by myself for over 30 minutes before I just decided to reschedule. No harm, no foul.

ALDERMANIC SIGNATURES

Just last winter, someone shot at me eight times. The first shot grazed the left side of my head and knocked off my White Sox hat. Before I knew it, I'd fallen to the ground. The next shot woke me up, and I got up and ran for my life. This winter, I'm back on the same block, coincidentally wearing the same jacket, while I'm collecting signatures to get our current alderman back on the ballot. Now, it wasn't my idea to canvass over here, but every member of the young Dems got a list of random registered voters, and we were assigned this block. My friend didn't want to canvass over here by herself, so she asked me to accompany her. I didn't even realize our destination until we pulled up to the block. The first thing that crossed my mind was that we didn't want to do this out here, on this particular block. But you do what you've got to do when you believe in something or someone.

This time around, I'm more aware of every car that passes by. As we were knocking on the door of a bungalow, I tensed up when I hear the loud rev of an old car's engine as it zoomed by at a high speed. I resisted the urge, or perhaps the instinct, to take cover behind the brick porch column. Then, ahhh, I sighed in relief as the car passed by without incident, just as a lady came to the window and peered through the blinds. I wondered if she saw what I was thinking.

"What do you want?" she asked through the window. I gave her the pitch, and she walked away from the window and came to the door. She looked at me through the frosted fiberglass front door windows and asked once again what I wanted. Now I have to convince her to sign the petition in a different way. It's all good. I get it. You've gotta be triple sure before you open your doors nowadays. She agreed to crack the door open.

IT'S NOT REGULAR

After signing the petition, she told my friend that it was good that she had someone walking with her. It ain't safe. I'm thinking, yeah, the same goes for me, too.

When people answer the door, I'm delighted because I get to be myself. Being able to talk with them takes my mind off my harrowing near-death experience last year. I talked with an old man who agreed to sign the petition, but he also wanted me to inform the alderman that the lights in his alley weren't working. It's pretty intimidating to go into a dark alley, he said. As he spoke, I was reminded that last year, just one alley down, I had to run for my life. My mind recalled the incident. With nowhere to run to, I hid underneath a porch because I thought the shooters were chasing me. When I made it to the alley, I shed my hoodie because I thought I'd need it for a tourniquet. Under that porch, I thanked God I wasn't shot.

Then, I snapped back into the present and agreed to let the alderman know about the lights.

As we walked off the old man's porch, a guy on a bike with a lady walking beside him approached. Instinctively, I asked him if he'd sign the petition. Out of everyone I'd met that day, he was the most willing to sign the petition. He needed no convincing. He understood the power of voting—I could just tell. He took the time to sign the petition, even though it was cold, and walked away, with his pants sagging so low his boxers were visible, and it didn't matter to him. There was no urge to pull them up.

I may need to get a concealed carry permit if I want to collect signatures to get aldermen on the ballot. It's important to me, but so is my life.

THE POWERS THAT BE

The powers that be came to my block last week—the news media.

I saw the camera man walk past a dollar lot that was transformed into a beautiful garden. Professionally landscaped, it included red lava rocks, an outdoor gazebo with a wooden stage, and a colorful mural on the back wall. The camera guy just walked past this oasis in Englewood, right in the middle of the block on 68th and Paulina, never even acknowledging the garden. Then he put the camera on his shoulder and pointed it at the one abandoned house with boarded up windows on the block. Curious, I asked what he was doing, and he said he was grabbing an exterior shot. When I asked what that was, he said an exterior shot is a television production term. It is a film or a scene shot outside. He stayed a few minutes, zoomed in and out a few times, and then walked north up the block.

As he was walking up the block, he walked right by a 50-million-dollar school, Myles Davis Academy on 67th and Paulina. This is Chicago's first children's engineering school and is rated Level One in CPS's school quality ratings report. The graduates from Myles Davis academy go on to some of the best high schools in the city. The camera guy walked right by it and headed for the alley. I then watched him put his camera on his shoulder, bend down, and focus on the empty liquor bottles and the trash in the alley. I asked if he was grabbing more exterior shots. He said no—he was grabbing B-roll. Explaining that it's another television production term, he described B-roll as supplemental or alternative footage intercut with the main shot. He was from a suburb but had gone to school at Columbia to study video production and was hired to tell stories by the powers that be, the news media.

Then he ran up the block to capture a group of youth walking by. So I asked if he gathering more B-roll, and he said no, he was getting an interview of auxiliary characters. When I asked what auxiliary characters were, he said they were blah blah blah, blah blah.

I only followed this camera guy around for ten minutes, but in that time, he's captured exterior shots of the only vacant home in the block with boarded up windows, B-roll footage of the broken bottles on the ground and the trash in the alley, and auxiliary character interviews of a group of guys with sagging jeans.

Why does this matter? Well, this story he was creating for the powers that be was going to be released at 9 p.m. that night to millions of viewers in Chicagoland Indiana area. So I waited for it. I set the TV to record it, because I try not to watch too much news. My mom watched enough news for everybody, but I looked forward to this one.

When this segment about 68th and Paulina aired, it was a gross misrepresentation, a parody, a spoof. There was no sign of hope on the block. There was no beautiful garden, there was no 50-million-dollar school, there was no block club. This wasn't news; it was propaganda created to scare people.

You may be thinking this doesn't matter to you because you don't live on the south side. Well, I'm telling you it matters. Don't believe me? Then go out of town and tell somebody you live in Chicago. They'll look at you like you're Al Capone. And you'll try to explain, saying you live on the north side or downtown or Streeterville. It won't matter; it's all Chicago.

Is Chicago a horrible place? Is the news telling the truth? Have we been deceived?

Who knows?

That's why it's important to separate reality from entertainment and step outside your comfort zone and experience and expose Chicago. Go grab a bite to eat in a community you never been to before. Get your hair and nails done in a new neighborhood. Look up from your cell phone and see what you can learn from different places and scenery. Like you'd study hard for an exam or work out hard in the gym, exercise your empathy. Once you do, you'll stop seeing yourself as 77 different communities and start seeing yourself as part of a greater whole. We are one Chicago. Post pics of yourself when you're out exploring because positivity beats negativity. Love outweighs evil every time.

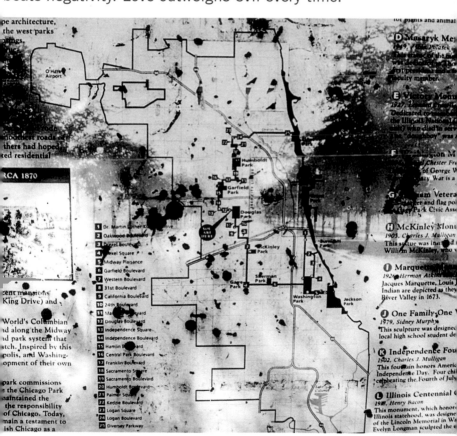

IT'S NOT REGULAR

DROP OFFS

You can say you have an after-school program that helps youth, but if you aren't taking the students home after your activities, you aren't really serving them. Are you going to expect parents to pick the kids up? You're a fool! Parents can't come pick their kids up at 9 p.m. It's too much of a burden. Asking them to do that would be like asking them for a million dollars, which they don't have. Are you going to ask the young ladies and young men to walk home through divested communities at night? Forget about it. I thought you cared about helping people. Do you really care about helping people, or do you care about a paycheck? You have to approach this work as doing more than people expect. That's why we do the night drop offs.

When the students are being dropped off at night, that is the only time they're comfortable enough to open up to each other and, sometimes, to me.

Most of the students stop at a house on the end of their block and pretend they have a phone call, because they don't want the other students in the van to see them walking to their house. They don't want the others to know where they live. Every guy does this. Not only do they fake phone calls, but when they get out of the van, many of them immediately begin to run through the alley, like they are running from a shelling, a bomb, or unfortunately, gunfire.

I have never worked with a student who has been able to pump gas. Not one single student, ever! None of them have ever pumped gas or learned how to do so. Using a debit card is foreign to them, as well. In the years I've been doing this, I haven't met a single student who has been exposed to doing either of these things. However, when I expose them to it, they find it to be an exciting experience and everybody wants to do it. (Interesting fact, none of the gas stations in the hood have any gas in the pumps, so even when you're teaching a kid to squeeze the nozzle, the gas drips out at a very slow pace.)

Gas and debit cards aren't the only things that people in the hood view and experience differently. Their language is unique, as well. In the hood, students use words like "hustle" and "work" to explain the act of selling drugs. The phrase "doing too much" is considered to be derogatory. It's literally a bad thing to be "doing too much." Gang members talk about each other like they're opponents playing a game against each other. They call each other the opposition, and their fellow gang members are all on the same team. Whites and blacks both use the N word openly. There's no hesitation at all when they see an "opp" or an opposition. You wouldn't even know who said it, either. But you would recognize the tone. The hate they use with the opposition almost gives it a familiar accent.

These students live different lives than people outside of the hood. Today, I heard a young lady say she thought a guy was really cute, but he wasn't her type. I thought that was a wise statement. What is her type? She might not even know, because like all of my students, she might not believe in the concept of love. None of my students believe in love, and they will admit that they don't. That word is off limits. If you use it, they'll say, "You're just saying things to be saying things." To them, love isn't real.

But love is real to me. I love my students, and I love this work, and one of the reasons is because of the drop offs, when they open up a little and let me see who they are. As I see their fears, their lack of belief in one of the biggest

IT'S NOT REGULAR

human emotions, their shame for their homes, and their lack of experiences that most people take for granted, I learn that they're teaching me just as much as I'm teaching them. When I drop them off after giving them new experiences, they let me into their world and expose me to things I've never experienced, as well.

I dropped a student off at her house the other day, and there was yellow crime scene tape wrapped around the alley on the side of her apartment. One of the other kids in the car said, "That's yellow tape, that's regular stuff. It ain't too serious because if it was serious, there'd be red tape. That's when you know there's been a shooting and there's a body." These were teenagers, and they're basically forensic scientists. Life had already taught them how to be immune to yellow tape. She got out the car, and we waited until she got in the apartment. This is a sign of doing more than what is expected to run an after-school program. Not only are we dropping the kids off at home after the educational exploration, (learn more about this in future chapters), but we also take the kids home after school.

COLLEGE DROP OFFS

This weekend, I dropped eight of my students off at Benedict College in South Carolina. It was a 20-hour drive both ways. As soon as I got back to Chicago, I teared up. I suppose I was crying because one of my students said I'm like a father figure to her. I always treat the explorers like family because I don't consider myself to be a non-profit executive. I don't do the program thing; I do the "really help out thing." My students know the difference. Mentoring isn't a job to me; it's a commitment to being a positive role model, adapting to whatever happens, and serving. So much stuff happens to students who grow up in under-resourced community areas. People in schools get shot, and parents get caught on drugs. One month, an electricity bill needs to be paid to keep a student's lights on, and another month, it's a phone bill that needs to be paid. Maybe they need an Uber ride late at night. There is always a need. This time, it was a ride to South Carolina. One thing you can't do is say, "Oh, I can't help you with this problem because it's not in the suite of programs I offer."

You also can't be in and out of their lives.

When I was growing up, if it weren't for a $500 limit credit card I got in the mail, I wouldn't have been able to get to college. My parents didn't have that kind of money. My father ended up getting a 17-foot U-Haul truck with a corn stalk graphic on the side, and we used my new credit card for gas money to get to Nebraska. I had no school supplies, and I couldn't afford any books. The back of the U-Haul was straight empty. I didn't want these students to have to go through something like that, so I told the principal if any students needed a ride to college, I'd take them. About 15 students needed help, so I'm out serving.

We picked the students and their parents up at 3 a.m. I swear, rats walk around like people at that hour. My mom always said that Chicago rats were as big as cats. I always thought she was joking until I drove down 16th and Kedzie at 3 a.m. When I saw what she was talking about, I just had to call my mom and share a laugh about it.

I told the kids to only bring one bag and we'd ship everything else, but they brought hampers and suitcases. As an organizer, you always have to expect that something won't go as planned. The new normal is adapting to whatever might happen. We just smashed as many bags as we could in the van and made it work. People had bags on their laps, under the seats, and in the aisle. This 15-passenger van was jam packed when we were ready to go, but my number one focus was making it to SC safely. This was a 15-hour journey, though, and the longest I'd driven before was only 10 hours, and that was way back in the day.

We drove through the concrete of Chicago, the cornfields of greater Illinois and Indiana, the blue grass of Kentucky, the winding roads and Smoky Mountains of Tennessee, and finally to the huge trees and humid weather of South Carolina. We didn't get there until about 10 p.m. because we encountered every type of element, except snow. Lord have mercy, things were so "elementy" out there.

We pulled up to campus and everything was everything. Benedict is an HBCU, so right away, we saw the drill teams and dancers in all white, pop locking and dropping. We saw the seniors welcoming the students. The football team players helped carry luggage up to the dorms. Gosh, I'd forgotten how big football players were. The orientation lines were very long, and the students all showed up in their latest outfits. People were from all over the world at Benedict College. One of the explorers was rooming with a young lady from Atlanta. The dorms weren't co-ed, and the RA's were a lot older. It almost seemed like they were professors. She told one of our explorers that she couldn't sag her jeans. I think that shocked her. I tried to turn around and not look, but the RA was right—in college, things are going to be different than in North Lawndale. You've got to adapt; it's good for you.

Right across the street from the college were row houses, low-income apartment buildings. They looked exactly like the Altgeld Garden Murray home projects, minus the steel doors. But, man, it literally was right across from the campus. I can already see my explorers organizing volunteer events and helping out. What's interesting is that Benedict College is in the same city, Columbia, SC, as South Carolina University. That side of town offers Polke Tuna restaurants, and on the HBCU side of town, there's low-income housing and community development corporations. I swear the contrast is pretty stark. Regardless, college is the truth.

Thanks to the donations that came in, we were able to buy the students basic things for their dorms. The parents and students were very grateful, but the parents were really extra thankful. They said so many prayers, thanking me. I prayed and said thanks for being in the position to serve. With the first part of the journey over, now we all have to learn how to support these students from afar. It was amazing to be there and witness everything.

The next trip planned was to another college in Southern Illinois. Please continue to support this work. Everything helps, and it makes a difference. You know, not having a way to get to college or basic supplies isn't regular, but here in Chicago, it is the norm. Together, we can change that.

When I see barbed and razor wire at the top of every business in the hood, I feel like I'm in jail. The use of such a preventative measure could also be seen as being detrimental to the neighborhood. Using other methods of crime prevention, such as trellis fencing and defensible planting, is often more effective and pleasant to look at.

WALK TO SCHOOL IN NORTH LAWNDALE

I unlock the deadbolt lock and the doorknob lock and open the door. I also pass through a steel gate that contracts like a slinky with the turn of another key.

Walking down the street, I've already noticed which cars belong over here and which cars don't. I'm aware that anything can pop off at any time. I'm the lookout. There's a Chevy with black tint, a baby blue Cadillac, a van with the curtains in it, a man with a motorcycle, a royal blue Acura, a Toyota Camry with a City College bumper sticker, a lady with a Cherokee, all black charger with silver rims, and a brown Honda minivan. Any car that pulls up that's not one of those nine, I say, look out. I'm the lookout on the block.

Breakfast is a bag of chips purchased at a corner store from one side of a panel of three-inch bulletproof glass that

IT'S NOT REGULAR

separates me from the cashier. I've become desensitized to the subliminal messages the community exhumes. It's regular. This bulletproof glass is a barrier between business owners and residents because, simply put, "It's not safe around here." Some business owners take the risk of not having bulletproof glass, but most prefer its protection. Their rational is that there's a good chance that someone in this neighborhood will try to rob them. In other words, no offense, but we don't trust you.

No offense is taken because the residents have long been desensitized to these precarious transactions. I often wonder how residents in Streeterville would feel if they had to order their Starbucks coffee through three-inch glass windows, or if they had to order their quiche through a bulletproof glass window. It'd be a great social experiment.

Of course, the bulletproof glass is just the tip of the iceberg. Under-resourced Chicago communities piece together injustices like Lego pieces, that when pieced together, end up being a bully named Society. At every turn, it reminds the youth how disadvantaged they are … how untrustworthy they are. After all, Society created this segregation. Society created these concentrations of poverty.

Youthful thoughts of joy are interrupted by someone yelling loudly and selling weed. I might buy some one day. My mother told me she hated me yesterday, Pops say he not a fine—he's experimenting, Mom's yelling at me, saying you'll be his mirror image. What's the worst that can happen?

Students are awakened from much-needed REM sleep by gunfire. Any desire to smile is discouraged because the block boys will think you're sweet if you don't walk with a scowl. When there's a lot of people to walk through, sometimes you'll see a right hand tucked in the front pocket of a hoodie to give the appearance of having a gun.

It's not regular in every community. It is here.

here's more technology on the light poles than there is in the classroom. Every other light pole in the hood has a blue light camera, a microphone at the top with a pop filter. It's called shot spotter technology. Using these microphones, the police receive instantaneous alerts of gunfire, which allows them to arrive at the precise location of a shooting event quickly. Look, I'm not throwing shade on the shot spotter technology, I just want you to envision what your kids are processing on the walk to school every day. These microphones also reassure communities that law enforcement is there to serve them and helps to build bridges with local citizens. It's actually the opposite, I feel like somebody's watching me and feel unsafe.

IT'S NOT REGULAR

LOOSE CHANGE MACHINE

On my way out of Jewel, I heard change jingling, and through the corner of my left eye, I saw a family waiting at the change machine for the pennies to count. Both of their fists were on the machine as they stared at it like they were looking at the results of a lottery machine. I remember looking for quarters and dimes on the ground as a child. I remember knowing that 50 cents meant a good dinner for me, because I could afford to buy myself two Little Debbie snacks, white zebra cake and an oatmeal pie.

Attention Shoppers!

Our shopping carts will lock if taken beyond the parking lot perimeter. While distinctive yellow lines mark normal exits, the entire lot perimeter is protected.

Nuestros carritos no funcionan fuera de los limites del estacionamiento. Aunque las lineas amarillas distintivas indican las salidas normales, todo el perimetro del estacionamiento esta protegido.

GATEKEEPER SYSTEMS

The picture is worth a thousand words. I mean the wheels lock up if you reach the end of the parking lot. Can they at least just donate a laptop to a school or something?

NON PROFIT LOCKDOWN

It looked like a small university as I pulled up, except there really was no way to walk up to a door and knock. All I saw were big black gates that had to be at least six or seven feet high. There was a little intercom at the front of the parking lot, so I figured I'd push the button. When I did, the big sweeping gate that lets cars into the parking lot opened up, and I walked through the parking lot into what seemed to be the main entrance. Damn, talk about security, I thought.

The front entrance was similar to the front entrance of a Chicago high school. You have to hit a button, and they see you on camera and buzz you in. Then there was a holding area that had another glass door with another buzzer on it. I could see the office workers on the other side of the locked door, and even they were enclosed to the right in another glass barrier. There were students on the other side of the door looking at me, wondering if they should let me in or not. Nobody did anything, so I knocked and pressed the button a few more times.

Finally, someone buzzed me in. I then walked up to the glass barrier; I don't think it was bulletproof glass, but it was still a barrier, and I told the secretary my name. She asked me for an ID and told me the person I was meeting would be with me soon. The guy came out pretty fast and greeted me, and we walked through another locked door to a smaller room to start our meeting.

This is a large non-profit in Chicago that works with youth.

Drug baggies lay empty on the earth. You can see them in almost every hood in Chicago. Not as abundant as dandelions, but definitely spread everywhere. Baggies on the ground that used to hold hope, those dissipated with the smoke.

BAGGIES

I smelled it from across the street. After running a mile, the smell of strong weed on 71st has you looking at everybody like they're the culprit. None of the people at the bus stop had blunts in their hands. When I arrived at the corner, nobody had weed, either. As I crossed the meter tracks to the south side of 71st Street, I heard an old man say, "Let me hit that. I know you know what to smoke." That's when I realized the man in a jacket about 10 yards in front of me was the smoker. His weed smelled fresh. The fact that a stranger asked him for a hit didn't shock me. There's a neighborliness in the hood. We all can relate to the struggle, bills due, family pressures, stress, no money—a few puffs of weed is like a vacation to Miami.

Politely let someone hit their blunt. There's a neighborliness here; people know it's hard.

Why am I sharing these incidents and situations? Why am I exposing the struggles and everyday life of the kids I serve? It's because I believe it's my duty to bring them to light so others can see things from a different perspective. If you don't see this stuff every day, it's easy to shrug your shoulders and act like it doesn't happen. It does though, and I intend to remain deeply connected to my community so I can continue to share my observations. I pray that God allows me to sustain this type of connection.

I don't wish for this book to be anything but a topical diagnosis about how to recognize the conditions that bring forth symptoms of hopelessness. All you have to do is open your eyes and see. There's a pattern that exists in divested community areas; I do my best to point out what I call societal jabs (hidden structural, economic, and government-induced oppression). There are times when people say, "I'm a product of my environment," and it sounds like an excuse. Well, I want to go into detail what people mean when they say "environment." That word encapsulates a lot. But I'm not one to stand back and just complain, so I'll try my best to offer some practical topical cures. I'm not about to go all psychological analysis on you. If my ideas spark any desire to take these findings further, by all means, get your Doctorate degree in these findings. That's up to you, but my purpose here is to serve, not analyze.

If we're the product of our environment, what happens if your environment isn't normal? How will that change and shape you? What impact will that have on your hopes and dreams, or will you even have any hope or dreams? How will it impact your opportunities, or will you believe that opportunity doesn't exist? When your environment is limited, even scarce, what does that mean for your future? What does that mean for the future of our youth?

It's not regular for a teenager who has grown up in Chicago to have never been downtown. It's not regular for kids to say they've never seen the lake. It's not regular that teenagers have never waved for a taxi or been on an elevator. It's not regular to have to become desensitized to gunshots. It's not regular that I have to sell hoodies and t-shirts to raise money for an after-school program that takes teenagers on educational explorations around the city of Chicago. Money should be in the city budget for things like this. It's not regular that I have to pay videographers a ton of money to highlight a teenager's fish-out-of-water experience when the students get on an elevator for the first time. This type of heartstring pulling has gained me national news attention. Some people see our testimonials and recap videos and say, "Wow, this is so heartfelt," and this leads them to donating. Others, though, turn a blind eye to the message they contain and say, "Jahmal you're so good at marketing. Who does your videos? I need them to shoot a commercial for my business."

It's not regular for a school to have 15 substitute teachers and only 15 teachers. It's not regular that King Drive is lit up with blue light cameras and helicopter lights, but during the holiday season, there are no holiday lights or garland on the poles.

On the Swisher Sweets wrapper, that conveniently holds two cigars, the warning label at the bottom is actually larger than the name Swisher Sweets. "Warning, Cigar Smoking causes lung cancer and heart disease." This warning may as well be invisible. It's hiding in plain sight.

There should be warning labels when you enter some Chicago community areas, like the big signs that say Streeterville or Rogers Park or West Loop. There should be a warning label when you cross 79th Street, and it should read, "Living in this area causes heart disease and worry." Whites have drummed up the term "food desert," because that makes the most academic sense. I hate that term because it's used to make sense to the people who don't live there. We're talking places that have no healthy eating options. You could call it Chinese food if you want to. But I've never seen a Chinese person eating Kams on 83rd. Have you ever seen a Chinese person sitting next to you in line to eat Chinese food? Like I said, there are no healthy eating options. Here, there are 25 barbershops and 35 churches. Our food options consist of chicken: Browns Chicken, Popeyes, Kentucky Fried, Churchs Chicken, and Sharks.

It's okay. We understand. It's hard out here. We got you. I just feel like it's cool to have Section 8, but can they have some community gardens in front of the properties, as well? Then residents could feel a sense of ownership and pride in their community. I also feel that if you own a building that has more than 20 units in Chicago, you should be required by law to have a doorman, security, or a camera. Something.

Real estate development is created without affordable housing, vouchers don't reflect the median fair rent price, and jobs have gone overseas. People who live in segregated communities without good access to jobs are more isolated than ever.

I saw a young man with shiny headphones rapping loudly, almost performing the drill rap lyrics, and I immediately knew he was in pain. He wasn't rapping his own lyrics. The music is therapy, especially when it's filled with excuses for why you are selling drugs, and why you are the way you are. Through the mistakes, you feel understood.

On Sports Center, they said Aaron Rodgers was a great quarterback because he understands situations. I can understand people, and I can understand the situations we can experience here in Chicago. Does that mean that if I can make it in Chicago, I can make it anywhere?

Survival isn't something most people have to think about on a regular basis. But for the students in our program and their families, it's something they don't stop thinking about. That must be a testament to their experiences. To survive means you're as experienced as Aaron Rodgers. You understand situations most people haven't experienced at all.

SURVEY:

Is bulletproof glass even effective? It's three inches thick. It can stop deadly force traveling at almost 2,000 mph, but what else does it obstruct? What else does it obstruct when it muffles the voices of two people talking to each other from opposite sides of the glass? What else does it obstruct when shop owners can't physically hand you what they're selling? In a world where people are hell bent on building walls, I challenge you to rethink: is bulletproof glass an assurance of safety or a barrier to trust? Help us understand the psychological effects of bulletproof glass by filling out this survey. This survey is also available digitally at itsnotregular. org.

1. To what extent does bulletproof glass in Chicago businesses promote more safety or more distrust in communities? *
More Safety
1
2
3
4
5
More Distrust

2. Describe how you feel when ordering your food through bulletproof glass, using any 3 words.
Example: disgusted, unwelcome, misunderstood, served, satisfied, unbothered
Your answer:

3. If you work in a service establishment, describe how it feels to serve customers through bulletproof glass, using any 3 words.
Example: inefficient, unnecessary, unkind, protected, unaffected, proud
Your answer:

4. Would you support a boycott on businesses using bulletproof glass?
Yes
No
Other:

5. Would you support a campaign to have bulletproof glass removed from major chain businesses?
Yes
No
Other:

6. To what extent does bulletproof glass make you feel safe?
Not Safe at All
1
2
3
4
5
Very Safe

IT'S NOT REGULAR

7. What would make you feel safe in lieu of bulletproof glass?
Your answer:

8. What age group are you in?
13 and younger
14 - 21
22 - 29
30 - 39
40 - 49
50 - 64
65 and older

9. In what zip code do you reside?
Your answer:

THE WHOLE POINT OF THIS BOOK

Growing up in these divested communities may lead to resilience, but all of this adds to the burden of being aware. This has broken their spirit, undermined their health, and robbed them of self-respect. It has destroyed their efficiency and employability. Families have been separated, and husbands and wives have divorced.

You don't realize how heavy that bag of burden is until you travel somewhere new. It may lead to heart failure and stress. Coupled with unhealthy eating, this is systematic oppression. When police pull up on people in these communities, they wonder why they are so hostile. Well, they almost have to be. The environment has messed with their well-being. They're all stressed out. Everybody is.

You can't live on the south side with all these key indicators without those things making the bag of awareness you carry at all times so heavy. You can't treat PTSD with liquid or weed. You can try, but it's not a good thing and will most likely make the problem worse. But yet that's our options. We don't have healthier or better alternatives. There is a liquor store on every street corner. I propose, however, that we need more CrossFit gyms, not more liquor stores.

I've gotten comfortable being uncomfortable.

ACKNOWLEDGEMENTS

S/o to all the coffee shops, which are really my living rooms in the city. I sit there and write and really listen to the sounds of the city. I love it. S/o to my family, Pops, Ma, Tiff, my daughters, Khammur and Kennedy, I love y'all. Huge shouts to my brother who put out a jazz album recently. Love you, man. S/o to my sister, Tay, we're both learning our own value. I think we lost the importance of this somewhere along the way. S/o to my man, 6lizz, 20 years, bro. Twenty year friends. S/o to my friend, Anthony Evora, thanks for letting me know the journey of this book was done, even if it didn't reach as many pages as I wanted it to be, sometimes it's good to be done. S/o to my man, Mony Mone. Salute, bro. My man, Nordy, and his mom, thank you for the love. Gotta say s/o to my team, C, Lady, Casey, Nathaniel, Ernesto, we're the best. My board members, Will and family, it's been a long time, man. Thank you for being on this journey with me, Will. S/o to Sam Hobert, Katie, love you, Ron, Alex, Andy, Jamal, Tristan, Vernee, Brandon, Len, Malcolm. S/o to Rahm Emanuel, appreciate you putting me on those stages. S/o to the Facebook team. S/o to Harley Goneso, love you. My man, Rich Grey, Fola Orokunle. Colin, even though you don't respond to my emails anymore, I still love you. S/o to Roseanna Ander, Marisa Novara, S/o to Patti McKenna and St!zo, this is our sixth book in ten years.

THE NEW PHILADELPHIA

I passed the new Philadelphia and pray that
God is helping us
Cash my check at the Western Union like it's regular
Order food through the bulletproof glass like it's regular
German Shepherds sniff me on the train like it's regular
Blue lights flashing on the poles like it's regular
Red X's on boarded up homes, that ain't regular
Shot spotters sit on top of poles like it's regular
Dead people still casting votes like it's regular
Garrets popcorn lines long like it's regular
Welfare line is long, yeah, yeah, that's every month
Ain't nobody in the line to vote, though, that's regular
Same alderman for twenty years likes it's regular
Cops shot him 16 times like it's regular
He didn't even get no jail time, that ain't regular
Every month another mass shooting getting deadlier
Passing by this church, I always pray that God is helping us

IT'S NOT REGULAR

Today we took a group of newly recruited police officers on a tour of a community they police. It's the North Lawndale community on the west side of Chicago, the same community Dr. King lived in when he stayed in Chicago. Similar to the time when King lived, the North Lawndale community is still a high poverty and high crime area.

I'm sure there's some reason for this. With over 5,000 international restaurants in 73 countries, a company worth more than 5 billon should be able to afford a couple extra rolls of toilet paper.

I run a non-profit organization, and part of what we do is take teenagers from communities like North Lawndale on educational field trips. We don't call them field trips; we call them explorations. You can call them whatever you'd like, though. I'm honestly tired of trying to sound and write smart to get grants or impress folks. What we do is incredibly simple, it's not easy, but it's incredibly simple. We take people out of their world so they can experience a far different world for the very first time.

At My Block, My Hood, My City (M3), we believe that if you

show someone better, they'll do better. If they don't know any better, they won't do better. In fact, if students don't see anything different and stay isolated in their immediate environment (in this case, the North Lawndale community), they'll grow up thinking poverty is normal when, in fact, it is not. If these students never left their environment, they wouldn't know that in many communities, it's not regular to see so many police officers every day. Essentially, what we do is expose these students from neighborhoods like North Lawndale to different cultures, different perspectives, and different foods. I started this organization right here in North Lawndale, and we've experienced a lot of successes.

In my previous book, Exposure is Key, I talk in depth about the Explorers Program, but I don't want to get into great detail in this book. This book is about re-sensitizing us from what has desensitized us. It's about realizing that just because something is the way it is, that doesn't mean we have to accept it as normal. It's about creating awareness, so we can aspire to be better as individuals and as communities.

Anyway, we created awareness in these newly recruited officers. We know that police officers are used to responding to people when they are in high-stress situations. Often, that's the only perspective they have of a community and the people who live in it. High-stress situations, however, create high-stress interactions. Our tour provided these officers with a different perspective. It was good for them to see the residents sitting on their porches and gave them an opportunity to greet them as they are. It's about understanding other people and building relationships. Sure, they might not walk in our shoes, but at least now they are getting to know the people who walk in them.

To know what's regular, sometimes people in the hood need

to visit downtown so they can see how other people live and work.

To know what's regular for us, sometimes we need others to come into our communities so they can see us and how we live and work, and so they can see our everyday struggles and environment.

Regardless where we live, we all deserve to have hopes and dreams. It's my vision that someday we all will. But on the south side, there's a lack of hope ... and that's not regular.

WEIGHTED BLANKETS

Many Chicago youth suffering from PTSD have found relief from weighted blankets. This fear of falling asleep affects day-to-day life. It can be hard to focus throughout the day, and, as a consequence, work and school may suffer. Those combating PTSD may be easily startled and lash out at friends and family. Designed to weigh 10% of your body weight, weighted blankets put gentle pressure on the body's sensory receptors. The feeling is similar to a firm hug, which provides a feeling a safety and relief.

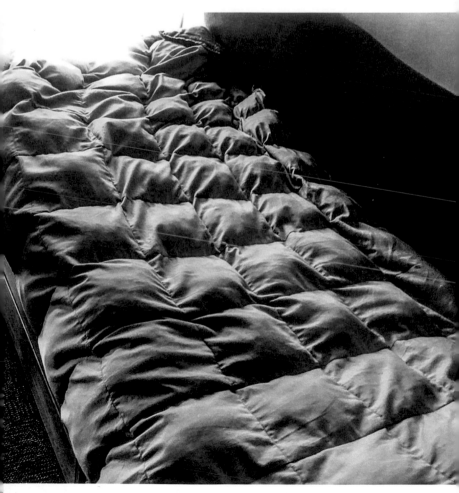

IT'S NOT REGULAR

A champion of social justice, Jahmal Cole's mission is to build a more interconnected Chicago on the pillars of service and education. As the founder and CEO of the city's fastest growing social impact organization, My Block My Hood My City, Jahmal is the creator of an exposure-based education program for teens and a network of volunteer initiatives that serve Chicago communities year-round. Traveling, youth mentorship and community organizing are the subjects of Jahmal's highly acclaimed books and speeches, He has spoken to audiences ranging from high school students to the Mayor of Chicago.

Jahmal is the recipient of the 2019 Champion of Freedom Award from Mayor Rahm Emanuel, the Chicago Defender Men of Excellence Honoree, and the Chicago City Council Resolution Award. He was also named one of the "20 Most Inspiring Chicagoans" by Streetwise Magazine and a Chicagoan of the Year by Chicago Magazine.